I0489942

27+ HACKS TO YOUR

FINANCIAL FREEDOM

◆ ◆ ◆

*Simple ways to start
saving, increase wealth,
and change your money
mindset for good*

Woke Money Hero

About the Author

◆ ◆ ◆

Anyone can start saving money and living the life they dream of. As a Money Coach and author, Woke Money Hero researches and develops courses and books on **how to shift your money mindset for good**.

Having grown up in the 1% but also having watched his father make poor investment decisions and lose it all, he has the unique perspective of how both worlds work.

The hacks and philosophies he implements are what helped him save $100K three times in his life, live off of passive income, and retire at age 37.

He got an early start as a real estate investor and FIRE (*Financial Independence, Retire Early*) advocate and combines his own experiences with proven money-saving hacks to provide clear guidelines and strategies to start saving money and living your best life.

If you live paycheck-to-paycheck and know there has to be more to life, he can help you break out of the habits that limit you by finally understanding why your relationship with money is skewed and the exact steps to take to repair it.

27+ Hacks to Your Financial Freedom:
*Simple ways to start saving, increase wealth, and
change your money mindset for good*

by Woke Money Hero

Kindle Publishing
Amazon Services LLC, 410 Terry Ave N, Seattle, WA 98109

www.WokeMoneyHero.com

Avatar Designed by macrovector / Freepik

Ebook ISBN: 978-1-79908-321-4

For my Dad who taught me there's no such thing as "can't"

Introduction

Part 1: Your Money Mindset

Part 2: Money-Saving Food Hacks

Part 3: Money-Saving Health Hacks

Part 4: Money-Saving Car Hacks

Part 5: Money-Saving Housing Hacks

Part 6: Money-Saving Entertainment Hacks

Part 7: Money-Saving Travel Hacks

INTRODUCTION

I'm going to make this Intro short and sweet: I'm Woke Money Hero and my aim in life is to give you the inside track to what makes some people financially better off than others. That's it. I do this by sharing my personal story. It's not to brag or to make you feel less than or more than, happy or sad, it's meant to inspire you to see the truth. The truth that has evaded you for so long about saving (and making) money. I don't use my real identity because I don't feel it's necessary: I don't need or want notoriety and I sure as Hell don't want the fame :)

What I do want is YOU to see the possibility of a new life. One that gets you what you want when you want it. And my hope is that by providing these hacks, you'll pay it forward one day and do amazing things. Not the things that bring you fame and fortune, those are great if you want them too, but the things that bring you happiness and peace. For what is life but time spent doing things you despise or doing things you desire?

And I realize charging so little for my book isn't going to make me a ton of money. That's perfectly fine by me.

If I can help even a handful of people to realize that they can have control over their money, I feel fulfilled. So thank you for trying to tackle saving money with me. I give you mad props. By the way, if you're over the age of ~45, you're not really going to get all the references to pop culture. Sorry about that :(this book is more for younger peeps but that doesn't mean you can't find value. On the contrary. I just don't have a translated version for you lol (I'm totally kidding). Ask a 40-year-old what they wish they had done when they were 30 and they will invariably say "save more money."

And in case you're wondering: this book isn't for people who have jobs where they're making large amounts of money and leading a privileged life, just needing a couple hacks to get them through to saving more than they already are. Far from it. Most books about money are going to appeal to a middle- or upper-middle class group of people for the simple fact that the author knows this group has money to spend! Are they really helping anyone? Sure. But are they really helping the people who really need help? The single mothers, the recent college grads, the person who just got laid off for the first time? I doubt it. I know my experience and knowledge can be put to good use by YOU.

That being said, this book is to the point. I don't like wasting people's time. And I can't stand someone droning on and on about themselves or how great they are. My own experiences are included to show *how* I did something or to show *why* I did them that way. My editor pushed me to do this. So please know that talking about myself is used sparingly and tactfully. Not everyone has had the privilege that I have had in life but not everyone has seen the opposite end of the spectrum and experienced their parents having to file for bankruptcy and moving in with their cousins either. I combine the money highs with the money lows to paint the whole money picture.

My promise to you is: by the end of this book, you'll know exactly why most people, including you, aren't able to save money – and more importantly, what you can do to finally take back control of your money and start the future you've dreamed of today. Let's go!

PART 1:

Your Money Mindset

CHAPTER 1:

*Why You Haven't Been
Able to Save*

Let's get something out of the way right from the start: you've been lied to! Not in a malicious or nefarious way. But in an "if you're a good person who does what they're supposed to, you'll get what you deserve" way. From a very young age, we're all taught that obeying the rules will get us what we want:

- At school, if we study hard, learn the lessons the teacher has prepared, and do well on their tests, we'll pass and get into good schools and get good jobs.
- At work, if we work hard and climb the corporate ladder, we'll get a promotion and earn more money in order to provide for our family.
- In life, if we buy products with our hard-earned money, we'll get the same happiness that our beloved favorite celebrities have.

And thus creates the hamster wheel that most people fall into; the rat race that no one ends up winning. If we deviate from what's expected, the worst things can potentially happen: we'll be all alone, we won't have any money, and we'll be laughed at by our peers or worse, our parents.

I'm here to tell you that is complete BS. There is another way. You just haven't been taught it yet. That's the purpose of this book, the purpose of my life, and what I truly hope you get out of reading this book: you are able to save money and live the life you truly want. **The trick is knowing the hacks to get there and understand what's prevented you before.**

Are rich people luckier or more ambitious than the rest of us? Or do they know something that we can learn? I've seen both sides of the coin: I grew up in one of the wealthiest zip code in the United States, went to private schools, country clubs, traveled around the world when I was 4. My Dad was a real estate investor and made some good investments and then made some very bad ones, and by the time I was 12, we lost everything: no more expensive dinners, no more fancy trips, and because I subconsciously tied my happiness to how much money my family had, no more friends or fun.

For whatever reason, when I was 13, I had a moment of clarity and made the decision that I was going to be successful no matter what. I remember it clear as day: I was standing in the driveway of one of my parent's apartment buildings that was going to have to be sold because my Dad said they were filing for bankruptcy and I told myself that I would never be like him and have to admit failure. I was determined to succeed in life.

Looking back, I now know why: my Dad is brilliant, but he made many financial mistakes, and I wasn't going to make the same mistakes that he did. And so started a journey that's spanned over 2 decades of finding the cheaper way to do things, the smarter way to get ahead, and the most efficient way to get what I want out of life. Little did I know at the time how impactful these events would be on my life. Ironically, admitting failure is one of the **most** important things you can do in order to be successful.

Adulting can be hard, I hear you. And I've been there: trying to budget, trying to save, trying to get a promotion. Working to put myself through grad school, trying to scrape together enough money for a $12 meal instead of my usual $3 Taco Bell run. But then I realized that if most people weren't able to save money, I needed to approach things a little bit differently than other people. And once I figured out the right formula, things really started to take off: I bought my first property when I was 26 and my next place 10 years later, renting out the first. Now I make enough money off the rental property to not have to work and instead, I do things that bring me happiness and then write about what I've learned for others to benefit from. I'm telling you this because I want you to finally see the truth about money. It can work in your favor if you take the right steps to first save it and then invest it.

And no wonder you aren't saving money: it's easy to get into debt! No one *wants* to get the generic ice cream just because it's cheaper; they want the real stuff but it may be too expensive. Consumer spending makes up roughly 70% of the economy[1]. It ain't cool to say "I can't go out this weekend because I'm saving up for a car." Or "Check out this old bed frame I scored on Craigslist." Would a celebrity do that? Would a rich person brag about it? I'm guessing not. All these influences: from the food industry, the health industry, the medical industry – you name it, they all make more money the more money you spend – have come together to "program you" and trick you into thinking you need and want more things.

Remember, they don't teach this stuff in schools:
- How to save money
- How to invest money
- How to retire early

That's because they don't want you to! If you stop buying things, you won't be making companies richer and you won't be paying more taxes. The government doesn't like that one bit. And they're going to make sure that you know it: why do you think it took consumer and advocacy groups to limit cigarette commercials or sugary cereal ads to young kids? Our government is "by the people, for the people". And those people include companies and special interest groups with very deep pockets who want you to spend more money. If you buy into that thinking, you've bought into a way of life that will keep you living from paycheck to paycheck, my friend

I know how awful that can feel. And I'm worried that you've been stuck in this pattern for far too long. As we get older, we get more set in our ways. We get so good at interpreting and anticipating events and people, that we develop habits in the ways we think. Thinking something like "saving money is for losers" or "savers aren't fun to be around" is probably something that you learned from a young age. Or at least an age when you were absorbing the thoughts and judgments of others. Have you ever stopped to think about why you thought that way? Could it be possible that saving money will actually get you what you want?

Maybe you know that saving money is a good thing. But you can't seem to wrap your head around where to start. That it's possible for others but not yourself. The actual change in mindset from someone who doesn't save to someone who does can cause stress. But where does this stress come from and how do we get around it?

Well, this question intrigued me so much that I spent months researching the answer and found that there is a way out of this trap – and it has all to do with how we think. We actually perceive the world through a lens of thoughts that are developed based on what we learn when growing up. If we learned that we are capable and competent as kids, we'll see ourselves as capable and competent adults. If we were taught from an early age that "money doesn't grow on trees" or "a penny saved is a penny earned", we carry that thought through to adulthood.

That, my friends, is why the rich get richer, why rich kids seem to more easily get ahead, why books like "Rich Dad, Poor Dad"[2] tell the truth: rich people do know something we don't – your mindset makes all the difference.

CHAPTER 2:

3 Ways to Start Changing Your Mind

There's good news and some more good news: the first set of good news is that even though we can't control what happens to us, we can control how we react to it. Even though we didn't grow up rich, it's OK to want to be rich and to be able to get rich. The other set of good news is there are key ways of thinking that we can learn in order to model how rich people got that way. If this is something that interests you, I want that for you too! If you want to learn how to make just enough to get by, we can do that too. It's up to you how much you want to save.

I know some of you are saying: I sure as Hell don't want to be a rich person who shits on other people beneath me. Again, that very likely is a mindset that you've carried from your younger days. Who says rich people can't be generous and charitable? There are countless foundations, causes, and organizations that rely on the generosity of wealthy individuals and families in order to operate.

Once you develop the skills to manage your money, you've gained an important skill for the rest of your life. While money can't buy happiness, it can sure help us influence our future, prevent or reduce stress, and if we want, we can end up sharing the wealth. Look at Bill Gates. Warren Buffett. Mark Zuckerberg (not the best example but an example nonetheless). Each of these men (who also happen to be a few of the richest men in the world), all have strict donation guidelines that they live by. They also get to write off the donations on their taxes (more on this in a later chapter), but the fact remains: if they kept all that money for themselves, their sphere of influence would be much smaller than it is.

Think different
If I could choose one shift in thinking to teach you, it is this: *if you want to be remarkable, give them something to talk about.* You don't have to live the life that others expect. You can break out of the mold that practically everyone else falls into. Instead of following the herd, what do YOU want to do? What help can YOU provide others based on your past experiences? What do YOU think you're good at and enjoy doing?

Looking back, I remember a time when I didn't know how I was going to be successful. But I knew that I was. I didn't know how I was going to save the money to get me the things that I wanted, but I knew that I could. I worked my way through grad school and I lived with my parents for a few years. If I told you those two things are likely 80% of the reason why I am where I am today, would you believe it? It's true. Sure, a lot of people work while going to school. But I did things a little differently than others. I literally couldn't do things the same way as others because that would get me average results. So knowing that having an MBA would make me more money in the working world and knowing that most people start working out of college and don't go back to get their Masters or life makes it too hard to do so, I set out to get my MBA degree right after college.

Doing it this way, I knew that I wouldn't be getting into a top school but that was OK by me – I was an above average student I guess but school was usually boring unless I was learning certain subjects like Statistics or Psychology. I just knew that having an MBA would make me more money so that's what I got.

And it paid off: I ended up getting a job making about $20K more than I would if I hadn't. I lost 2 years in the working world, yes, but starting out earning $20K more meant that for every year after, I was $20K ahead. And let me be clear: I wasn't an Engineer or a Software Developer earning the big bucks. I went into Marketing and more specifically Marketing Research – a specialty that not a lot of people go into (hope you're noticing the theme). But that meant being able to land a job more easily and more job security when I got it.

During that time of my first job, I also did something that more and more people our age are doing these days: rooming with Mom and/or Dad. Just a few years ago, this idea carried with it an intense stigma – a pitiful "poor Johnny, he had to move in with his parents" stigma. But no longer – it has become a way of life. A necessary evil to save money. And it wasn't so bad. I had my own space and did my own things, saving 95% of my paycheck. If I hadn't done that, it would have taken me many, many more years to save enough for a down payment for a house. And I just happened to buy in one of the most expensive cities in the country.

What do YOU want?

Think big

Why did I choose one of the most expensive cities in the country to buy a condo? Well, if you look at the bigger picture, you see that my plan was starting to form: I would eventually find a woman to marry and move away together, thus receiving a very high rent payment for my place. The rent would be able to cover the mortgage, the taxes, the expenses, and half the mortgage at a new place. All set. No need to work. My property was working for me.

So often we're caught in the endless loop of "I need this much to live" and then you make that much. And then the cycle repeats with spending even more money. I can't tell you how many people I've worked with that revert to this thinking. There's a reason: most people do this and most people get average results.

If I had just one more thing to choose to teach you, it would be to think BIG. If you need $2,000 per month to live, trick yourself into thinking that you actually need $2,500. Where will the money come from? That doesn't have to be your main concern from the start. Your mind will come up with ways. Don't worry, I'm going to show you in the coming chapters how to find extra money by not spending it on things that you don't actually need.

But how do you start to think big? What can you start doing now? There is a hack that you can start using right now to trick your brain into thinking that you don't have money to spend and it involves setting up an automatic deposit to your Savings Account and literally doing nothing else. Just let it sit. Out of sight, out of mind.

The trick is that your brain will start to think that that money really isn't available to spend. My Savings Account was literally 20 miles away. In my mind, in order to get the money out, I had to drive 20 miles to get it. Why the heck would I do that? Of course, I could have found an ATM and could have withdrawn cash, but it was a credit union (did I mention they have better savings rates than larger banks and I worked at a credit union in grad school so I knew how the system worked?) so I had to figure out where to find an ATM and

I just didn't bother to.

Combining the automatic savings of my paychecks with the house hack of living with Mom and Dad, I was able to save $100K in just under 3 years at the age of 26. Not bad. The interest on my savings was literally paying for my educational loans by the end. And I didn't have any expenses because my parents weren't charging me for living with them. I am 100% aware that this is not always the case. Some parents think that charging their kids for living with them will teach them how to save money. But, if you approach the situation a little differently, do you think maybe your parents could be open to the fact that by not charging you, you're actually learning a ton more about controlling your own money and having exponentially more savings power to move out quicker? Or putting the rent you pay them in a fund for when you move out?

I get it – some parents just can't see past the fact that you're not out on your own yet. And maybe you'll have to pay them a little rent for a time. But maybe that'll be the little bit of extra money that you can save that you'll use to move out and get a roommate in your own place. I definitely go into more details about how to make this situation work out for you in a later chapter.

What I want you to get is that saving money can be as big or as small of a task as you want it to be. How do you eat an elephant? One bite at a time (please don't actually eat an elephant). Saving is a way of thinking that will, in time, become a system. There are clear steps and very clear actions that can greatly increase your chances of success. This is the very reason I was able to save $100,000 three times in my life and retire by age 37. That's the big "secret".

Think smart
We come to the final mindset shift that I would teach you if I could only give you 3. This one is more of a lifestyle shift, not just a mindset shift. And it's probably the hardest one to tackle. That's why the rest of the book is going to help you master it. It's all about finding frugal ways to do the things that you need to do and then making them into a habit. And let me be crystal clear: there's a difference between being cheap and being frugal. Being cheap means that you are only interested in finding the cheapest products/services. Being frugal means that you are interested in finding good products/services cheaper. Small switch, big difference!

Sure, you've probably read about "how to save money" before. But all that advice is readily available to anyone on the internet. Chances are you've tried these things and revert back to your old ways at some point. I chose to give you the real deal – the stuff no one is talking about. The hacks to getting what you want for less money by changing your thinking. Not fighting the urge to spend money but *replacing* the urges with more helpful, efficient ways of doing things.

Things like how to get cheap or even free online courses. No one is talking about that. You know why? Because that would mean a "guru" isn't making money. Well, I did a ton of research on these Marketing "gurus" and only a select handful are legit. I watched over 30 webinars from these guys! And only chose to reach out to 2 of them. I learned more from them than all the other 28 combined. And guess what? One of them gave me their course for FREE. More on how to do that later.

Another area where I'm pretty passionate about is cars. If you're like me, you've got your favorites. I'm into the classics – Mercedes to be exact. Old school cars come with their share of needed fixes but if you're into repairing and upkeep, it can become a less-expensive hobby by saving you on auto body shops. YouTube instructional videos are also a major value-add when it comes to learning things for free. That's how I've designed my YouTube channel "Woke Money Hero" – a place where you can learn a ton of hacks on saving money and then put that money to work for you. Do I make money off of the videos? In a roundabout way, yes, of course. But I'm going to show you how to do that too.

Thinking smart about money is all about noticing opportunities where others cannot see them. Some people clip coupons. That's nice but that's not efficient. It also isn't going to get you the big savings that doing other things like budgeting will. Let me ask you a question: who makes more money – the person who makes $60K per year and has $20K in expenses or the person who makes $80K but has $45K in expenses? Depends on how you define "making money". In my book, the more you save, the more you earn. And the more you earn, the more investing power you have which is where the real magic happens.

CHAPTER 3:

Money-Saving Hacks to Live By

Here's the thing: you can do your own research and find money hacks on the internet. I just did. There are ways to make your own cleaning supplies (that was actually useful but I won't talk about it here) but that's been covered like 10 Million times before. There are sites to find coupons but who wants another chore to do? I don't see the value in writing a book about "hacks" that have been "hacked" before. You deserve better than that. Plus, you may have already tried them and they worked for a time but then they stopped working or you stopped working them.

My job is to show you *why* you haven't been able to save. To help you peer into your mindset to see what could have caused you to think that this hack wouldn't or couldn't work. And THAT I can assure you has not been done before. Think of it like your first money therapy session. I'm not a therapist, but I am a Money Coach and Founder at www.wokemoneyhero.com. Your first lesson is to start to think critically about what you spend your money on. Not like what everyone else thinks about when they think about spending money. You know better than that by now – do what others aren't doing. Moving forward, we're going to ignore a lot of the conventional wisdom (which is really just dressed up basics everyone already knows anyway). If others are budgeting at the beginning of the year and then unable to save money by February, be the person who figures out their budget for the year and then realistically readjusts at the beginning of the next month but always with the 2 end goals in mind: 1) How much do I want to save? and 2) What do I want to do with that money to help my life expand for the better?

The following 6 parts are broken up by all the hacks to save money in your life and the reasons why you may not have been able to save money in the past. Knowing the why behind why something didn't work is very powerful indeed. Think how powerful that is for a second: no one has made you do this before and it could be the very thing you need in order to really start saving money for your future. Today is the day that you take back control of your money.

On their own, each part has the potential to save you hundreds of dollars. Combine all the parts and some may call you a legit next-level saver. **I'll call you a Woke Money Hero**.

PART 2:

Money-Saving Food Hacks

When you look at what you're spending the most money on besides rent, is it food? If not, I bet it's pretty high up there. And it makes sense: after providing shelter for yourself and your family, you need to feed the beast that is your hunger in order to survive. And you'll likely eat more food and/or protein shakes if you start a really intense workout routine. So saving money on food is pretty important if you want to start this saving-money journey with me. So I've laid out the plans and the thinking that will get you on the right track. The first step is grocery shopping.

CHAPTER 4:

Grocery Shopping

Growing up, going to the grocery store was pretty fun, I have to admit. It was the '80s and packaged food was enjoying its heyday. The sugariest cereals, the fattiest cookies, the most convenient microwavable pizzas. We're talking an MTV's "Jersey Shore" Thanksgiving feast. There were also the health foods that were starting to come en vogue. "But that crap will kill you," my Mom would say. "All those chemicals."

So I stuck to the essentials: cereal, cookies, chips. Anything that tasted good and wasn't labeled "Diet" is what we'd get. Cost didn't matter. This was before my Dad lost everything and we had to watch what we spent. But when that change came, my Mom went from "get the real thing" to "get the cheap thing". And I subcon-

sciously held onto that belief for years! **You don't realize why you act a certain way until you stop to really
think about what caused it.**

Do you go to the grocery store with the thinking that
you can get whatever you want because you work hard
and you don't have the time to pick out the cheaper
or healthier option? What about the thought that coupons are for cheapskates? Maybe your Dad made a com-
ment once about it. Or you saw a show on TV and they
made fun of the old lady clipping coupons, holding up
the checkout line. I literally was in the grocery store
yesterday when I overheard this conversation: the hus-
band was telling his wife about the "super couponer"
ahead of him and his wife chuckled. We've all been
there. Why can't they move faster?!?!

But what if I told you there was a more efficient way
to get healthy food cheaper than what the majority of
people do or know about? Most people either go to
the store a couple times a month and bulk up thinking they're saving money (need a Costco membership?
Ask your mother :) or they run to the corner store only
when they need stuff and eat out the rest of the time.
How are most people doing with saving money? I can
assure you not that great. According to CNBC, the me-
dian U.S. household currently has less than $12K put
away between bank accounts and retirement savings.
And young people have much less[3].

The Hack: most fresh food spoils in a week. Use this

fact to your advantage by scheduling a food service to deliver this fresh food to you once a week. It's not as expensive as you would think: companies Amazon-Fresh, Thrive Market, and Good Eggs actually make their money the longer you stay with them. Trust me: I've compared the numbers. If you buy groceries in bulk, how many times have you thrown out rotten food? That's literally money down the drain. If you're running to the grocery store more than a couple times a week, think of how much gas you're wasting. By only getting what you can eat in a week, you're limiting the number of resources that you're wasting. Plus, you're planning ahead for the food that you normally would eat and making it more into a system: things like lettuce, bread, milk. You know you're going to eat it. The better you are at predicting these costs, the more light years ahead you'll be than your friends who are struggling to plan these things on their own. Again, it's an automatic system to help you save money.

Why this hack hasn't worked for you: You probably thought you had to do this all on your own. How much does that suck? No one taught you how to grocery shop. Maybe you went with your Mom growing up but it was always a chore to have to do. Your Mom seemed stressed and there was always an agenda, an item that wasn't on sale, or a fruit that wasn't ripe enough. What a hassle. "Ugh, I have to go to the grocery store. F it – I'm ordering in." "Ooh – wait. I can order my groceries on AmazonFresh. But crap, there's a minimum and I have to order extra stuff I won't eat! Boo."

You catch my drift. Make things easier on yourself. By looking at what you normally eat, you can save a bunch by not ordering more than you need. Simple hacks like:

● Buy a bag of nuts that you can divide up over the week into Tupperware to take to work instead of a bag of individually wrapped small bags of nuts that cost more.

● Buy cereal as it comes on sale. Cereal can last in the pantry unopened for weeks.

● Pop your own popcorn in a brown paper bag in the microwave and add all the crazy toppings you want.

● Oftentimes, a whole chicken costs less than the sum of its parts. The store simply charges more for cutting it up for you.

● Ever had homemade corn tortillas? Your life will change when you do. Buying ingredients like ground masa at your local Mexican market and making things like fresh tortillas at home instead of buying them pre-packed are healthier, often-times tastier, and will help you save.

CHAPTER 5:

Eating Out

I know what you're saying: buying groceries is good and all but I like to eat tasty food and go out to good restaurants all the time. I got you. Trust me. I'm a foodie through and through. It's my Mom's fault really lol. She was a good cook and my wife is a great cook. And her Mom is a good cook. I'm surrounded by food every time I go home. But eating out is a treat. I've been to all the newest restaurants and my wife even has her own blog about food, used to work in Napa Valley wine country, and has appeared on a restaurant review show in the Bay Area. We know good food.

As you also know, eating out can get pricey. Going out to eat with friends can get tricky when splitting the bill and then there's the Birthday dinner: paying for a friend at a pricey restaurant as a gift. Remember, it's more of the experience that you're paying for so plan accordingly.

The Hack: sites like Groupon provide things like half off deals for local restaurants and is usually a good place to start if you're ordering pizza. Taking things up a notch, sites like Caviar, DoorDash, and Uber Eats deliver restaurant food and there are always deals for first-time users. Need a coupon code?

● Sign up for a site called Honey – it aggregates coupons and tries them for you automatically. Works for Amazon too. Why pay more when you can use an online coupon and save?

● Not saying I indulge in this but one way to get around not having a coupon or being considered a new user on an account that you've already ordered from is to create a new email account and sign up again. Check the Terms of Service to make sure they'll accept the new email but same home address.

Why this hack hasn't worked for you: do you like playing by the rules? Chances are you'd never think of gaming the system. I truly believe I was born to find ways to game the system (legally, of course). Once there was a Groupon to my favorite pizza chain. And another Groupon for the same chain in another city. How'd I get half off pizza for 3 months straight? I simply planned ahead. The other city happened to be on my wife's ride home from her job so combining her Groupon account with my Groupon account, we were able to get pizza from both locations 2 times each. That's a lot of pizza. But it's seriously the best pizza.

Hate printing out coupons and handing them to your waiter? Groupon has a lesser known program called

Groupon+ (Plus) that ties to your credit card and gives you cash back. You have to claim the deals but it's some serious cash savings. Groupon also puts out $10 off deals every now and again. Plan ahead and you could get some unique holiday gifts checked off your list early.

CHAPTER 6:

Eating at Home/Work

Now that you've had all the pizza your heart desires, you're looking for a salad but paying $10 for one seems not only ridiculous, it now seems preposterous. I did the math: making your own salad saves you like $9 out of that $10. It's simple: making things at home saves money because you're buying in bulk for yourself. Restaurants make money by buying in bulk and upcharging for the preparation and service.

But don't fret if you aren't the cooking type. Remember: I'm not either. Aside from marrying a chef, there are tools to make you a home-chef hero: one of my favorites is the Instant Pot. This little gadget seriously ups your game by quickly cooking food in one pot. There are a ton of recipes and instructional videos on how to do every dish under the sun. For like a $100 investment, this one pays dividends.

Some other tools I swear by: a coffee or Espresso maker, SodaStream, and outdoor grill. If you're buying coffee from a coffee shop every day, I totally see why: it's convenient, they do it exactly how you like it, and it's not that much, right? Correct. Except when you do the math. Did you know that grabbing a latte at Starbucks every day is like a $720 habit? Always think in terms of a year. If you wouldn't shell out that kind of money all at once, then your habit needs hacking. Did you know you can get a good Espresso maker for way less than that? And it tastes great – just how you like it. Same deal with soda. Being able to control the sugar content is key and making it just as bubbly as you want it helps you save major moola. I included an outdoor grill because duh. SO good. And cheap. And easy. If you're living in an apartment, try a George Foreman grill or a Cast Iron Lodge Pan to grill up steaks.

The Hack: eating at home doesn't have to be a drag. You can make things easier on you by buying affordable kitchen gadgets that do most of the work. By DIY'ing dinner, you're able to control the ingredients, the cost, and the flavor. You may soon prefer eating in over eating out if you could just get that air fryer to make healthy treats...

The real hack here is to not make yourself feel bad unnecessarily if you want a fried treat every now and then. As long as you're saving elsewhere, **IT'S OK TO INDULGE SOMETIMES**. If you don't want to live like you're depriving yourself of a latte at Starbucks, get a latte at Starbucks! Life's too damn short. By now, you've learned that you can get what you want with the right mindset. A few dollars spent isn't going to break the bank. Especially when you have your big goal in mind of what you want your future to look like. You get to define that.

Why this hack hasn't worked for you: do you consider yourself a bad cook? Did you grow up never learning to make food for yourself? Are you comparing your dinner to what your BFF ate on Instagram? I guess there are people who can't learn how to cook but it's unlikely that you're completely helpless. With the amount of YouTube instructional videos out there, you'd be hard pressed not to find something you could make on your own. If you're looking for home chefs, I know Chef John and he's top notch.

I'd like to propose a challenge to you: try cooking at home just 2 more times than you usually do. The amount of money you'll save over the course of a month is truly shocking. If you're eating at home 3 times a week and up that to 5 times a week, you've increased your home meals by 60% thus increasing your savings accordingly.

And this doesn't just apply to dinners: try the same strategy for your work lunches. Or better yet, make it a plan to take your dinner leftovers to work. Your co-workers will be impressed by your skills. If they aren't, you can secretly laugh at them for spending so much money eating out.

PART 3:

Money-Saving Health Hacks

Now that we've gotten how to save money on food out of the way, the natural next step is to save you money on all things health-related. This will include things like working out, eating right, and making sure you're saving on insurance.

CHAPTER 7:

Working Out

Ever hear about how enrollment at gyms skyrockets like crazy come January? That's because everyone is making their health-related New Year's resolutions. Want to know what happens come February? Gyms are still making money because people signed up for a monthly membership with a steep cancelation policy. But they aren't making it to the gym as much as they were at the beginning of the year. Sucks for them, but gyms love it. **It's estimated that 80% of gym members do not use the gym on a regular basis**[4]! AYFKM? How's that for a company with a passive income model? The weight loss industry is designed to keep you on a tread-mill of money spending.

The Hack: One way to get around this entirely is to buy your own exercise equipment. You accomplish a few things by going this route:

- You save a ton of money for sure. Let's figure your monthly gym membership is around $50 (in major cities, that doesn't get you much). That's $600 that you're maybe or maybe not using. $600 can buy you a very nice treadmill that you could use whether or not it's raining. No random people's sweat, no waiting in line to use it.

● You save time. No more driving to the gym and waiting around for equipment when you could hop on your treadmill and get your workout out of the way.

● If you don't want to buy a new treadmill, what about buying a used treadmill for $200 on Craigslist/Nextdoor, or buying exercise bands, or weights/a yoga mat for YouTube workouts? A lot of people live in small spaces so don't have space for a treadmill.

Why this hack hasn't worked for you: "How are people going to check out my fine abs?" you think. Or "I'm not working my core as much on a treadmill." OK, 2 things: 1) who cares what people think? and 2) ever heard of doing sit-ups? Just saying there are ways around going to the gym to work out. One of my favorite things to do is hike: it's free, it's beautiful, and it can be quite a workout especially if you have a dog who likes to run. Do what works for you.

If biking, hiking, running, walking all don't cut it for you and the gym is part social activity for you, I can see you justifying the cost but there are still ways to get around the full cost of a gym membership. Costco sometimes has deals if you do a 2-year membership and health insurance companies are even paying parts of memberships if you can prove that you go regularly.

Check the specifics of your plan. Most people assume that they don't qualify or don't know how to check. Don't be one of those people. You're in control of your health, your money, and the decisions that you make to live a healthier lifestyle.

CHAPTER 8:

Eating Right

So you have your workout routine down but realize that you need to eat more now that you're lifting major poundage or running totes mileage. How do you eat healthy without breaking the bank? You've come to the right place, my friends. I've got the hacks and the reasons why you may think you aren't able to tackle this one below.

Let's take a step back and really define what healthy eating is. I think of it either in terms of organic foods or lightly processed food. It can be both. Generally speaking, the more organic you get, the more expensive. That's because of many different factors; the biggest probably being that organic food isn't mass produced. You get fewer toxins and potentially more taste and nutrients. That's a big generalization but you get my drift. And I'm not one to judge if you go that route for political and/or environmental reasons. Basically, if you want to eat organic on a tight budget, you very well can for sure. You just need to allocate a little more in your budget for grocery runs or deliveries.

If you're lucky enough to have farmer's markets in your area, this can be a great place to pick up your fruits and vegetables. One hack I like to do is only bring cash (some vendors accept Square payments etc.) and only keep it to either $20 or $40 total. That's because the bulk of my fruits and vegetables can still come from the grocery. Farmer's markets provide fresh produce BUT there have been stories about some shady vendors going to a local store, buying inventory there, and then selling it for a markup at farmer's markets. I'm not saying this is the rule, I'm saying it's the exception. But it brings up a great point: how do you truly know what you're getting? Oftentimes, the apple I'm eating from the Farmer's Market tastes just as good as one from the store. Just make sure you're buying from a certified farm with certified organic produce.

Another way to get cheaper healthy food (don't laugh) is to grow it. I know, I know – that's the lamest idea I've ever heard. But not really. We grow our own kale. It's not going to provide us food every week. But it is a nice treat now and again and is kind of like a built-in insurance policy: if we ever forget to order it one week, or want extra, instead of rushing off to the market, we can just grab it from the yard. Other fruits and veggies that do well for this kind of value add-on are:
- Carrots
- Tomatoes
- Oranges
- Lemons

• Limes

Just think of all the Tom Collins and Gin & Tonics you could have at home now with the ingredients in your backyard :) If you're low on outdoor space and/or live in an apartment, you can grow basil and fresh herbs on your windowsill. That save $ too.

The Hack: eating right is entirely possible even on a tight budget. The key is to plan ahead and look for value. Comparing prices between organic and non-organic is one way to accomplish this but again, if being organic is important to you, just allocate a little more money to your grocery budget. Cooking more at home will help with eating healthier as well.

Why this hack hasn't worked for you: this may sound harsh, but I didn't get to where I am by being meek. If you're tied to labels, you may have a harder time buying regular produce if you typically buy organic. And that's OK. Just know you will be paying more for groceries. If you haven't started eating healthy and go for more convenient options, that's OK too, but you'll feel much better if you take the steps to eat cleaner. Your mood and your waistline will thank you later too.

CHAPTER 9:

Health Insurance

I'm only going to briefly hit on health insurance. If your work pays for it, you need to be on it. And you need to go to both the doctor and the dentist. No exceptions. Putting off regular trips only increases the likelihood that issues will start to show.

The Hack: make sure you know what's covered and what's not. You have every right to know before you go in to either the doctor or the dentist how much the charges will roughly be and compare that to your deductible amount or the amount that you will need to pay out-of-pocket. Don't make the mistake of assuming something's covered if it's not. This could add hundreds or thousands of dollars unnecessarily. And don't assume that all doctors and dentists cost the same. Far, far from it. Be your own advocate.

If you're young and have no health concerns, I wouldn't advise getting the "most expensive" health plan. HMO's are typically better value than PPO's in general. If you want to take things up a notch, use an FSA (flexible saving account) or an HSA (health saving account) for co-pays or splurge for a massage if it's covered. That's pre-tax money so you're saving. But be aware: FSA's don't carry over to the next year so this is where knowing what you're really going to be spending on counts.

Why this hack hasn't worked for you: we all grow up thinking that doctors are the smartest people in the room. When they say something, we listen. But that can't always be true. For example, they don't know how you feel unless you tell them. Just because they say you need a procedure or need to take a particular drug, doesn't mean it's true or that you can't get a second opinion. Even if they say you need a drug, that doesn't mean there isn't a lower cost, generic version that will do just the same things. Stop blindly believing what doctors tell you. You will pay more than you need to in some cases. I have fallen for this several times. It wasn't until I started being my own health advocate that I got the true meaning of pushing back. It's worth it. Be sure you have faith in your doctors and dentists, just come with a tiny bit of healthy skepticism. It's worth the cost to have reputable ones and not try to find the cheapest ones on Yelp.

PART 4:

Money-Saving Car Hacks

Get ready for the "coolest" chapters: the chapters on cars! If you don't like cars, these chapters are still cool unless you don't have a car. Congrats, you can skip ahead. I've never bought a new car in my life. There's a reason...

CHAPTER 10:

Buying a Car

We've all heard that saying "if you buy a new car, you lose value just by driving it off the lot." And it's entirely true. Well, partly true at least. Let's say you buy a new car with the sole purpose of renting it out. Then what? Has it lost its value? What if you were able to make more money than the car payment and insurance cost? Now we're talking. The same goes for a house: a house is a liability until you rent it out and make money off of it. Then it becomes an asset. That's the part of the story that most people miss.

The Hack: Buy used. Or don't buy at all but definitely don't buy new or lease a car. Plain and simple. Of course, make sure that you aren't getting a lemon or one that has a bunch of work that needs to be done. I've made this mistake before. You can get around it by asking the seller to get an inspection (just like buying a house) from a reputable car repair shop. If you end up buying the car, you can work out a deal to split the cost of the inspection for example. "A used car is just like a new car – it's just older, wiser, and more needy."

There are tons of ways to find very good used cars. You can go the traditional route and look on popular sites that buy, sell, and trade cars. Or you could even look around your neighborhood. When I had my '78 Mercedes, I got a couple notes with phone numbers on my car asking if I would ever consider selling. These people could be collectors or passionate about a particular type of car and willing to spend top dollar. Or you could find someone willing to sell their car at a loss just to get rid of it. You never know unless you ask.

Why this hack hasn't worked for you: if you think the only way to buy a car is to go haggle with the new car dealership, I'm sorry to break it to you but that's not the right way to save money. Think outside the box and see if you can get the same car just a year or 2 later. Or make plans to rent it out on a site like Turo. Likewise, don't lease a car. The payments are high and you don't end up owning anything. It's the equivalent of charging something expensive on a high-interest credit card and then returning the item without getting a refund!

Instead, apply the loan that you were going to use for the new car on a used car. There are loans out there that start at an extremely low interest rate. It would be like getting free money to borrow against. Best of all, if you maintain the used car, you yourself could always end up selling it at a later time and recouping a portion of your expense. Literally thinking outside the car box.

I actually went for years living in the big city without a car. That may not be possible for you if you commute far to work or live outside a metropolitan area. But, if you have a public transportation system that you can take advantage of, you're going to save more than just gas: once you add in registration, insurance, and wear and tear, having a car is expensive. I ended up selling my old Mercedes and used the money to go to India, Thailand, and Bali. My car wasn't being driven enough because it was easier to take the bus or a train everywhere. Just consider it if it's something that you could potentially do. You'd definitely save a lot of cash on parking tickets :/ (try to avoid these at all costs, of course!)

CHAPTER 11:

Renting Out Your Car/Garage

Ever rent a car from the airport? Ever wonder why it's more expensive than other places to rent a car? That's because demand is the highest at the airport. They're able to get top dollar because the demand is constant so the supply needs to be there to meet these needs. Some people don't book ahead and need a car last minute. Sharing economy companies have realized this fact and banked on the fact that people will need to rent cars at the drop of a hat. Renting your car out can make your car payments more affordable. But it's not for everyone. We rented out our car a couple of years ago for a couple of months. Everything went fine, but it was just a little nerve racking. I'd suggest not renting out a new car either. Your anxiety would be through the sunroof.

The Hack: rent out your used car whenever you aren't using it. Another hack is renting out your garage when you aren't using it. We park our car in the driveway so there's always extra room in the garage. We've had a renter for several months. He's a car dealer who lives in the neighborhood. The original plan was he was going to be moving cars in and out of the garage a couple times a month. But I knew that was going to get old after a while and he'd likely just leave one car in there. It's free money – I don't have to do a thing.

Ever had a storage shed? The same thinking applies: they make their money off the fact that people forget about their things. Don't let this happen to you. I strongly suggest downsizing instead of paying for a storage shed. If you must get one, make sure you pay your bills every month. I've heard horror stories about storage companies selling people's possessions if they're past 45 days on the bill. No joke.

Why this hack hasn't worked for you: maybe you're emotionally tied to your things and feel the need to hold on to them no matter what. Maybe you moved around a lot as a kid and never could keep things that you cherished. Whatever the reason, getting over the need to have things is huge. The worst case scenario, of course, is what if a fire wiped out all your possessions? What do you have now that could and could not be replaced? What could be sold or donated?

Being able to think in terms of what money you could be making by doing without something or by turning a liability into an asset isn't easy. It takes years of practice and the courage to see it through. Are you willing to take that leap?

CHAPTER 12:

Car Insurance

Again, I'm not going to go too far into detail on this one because if you drive a car, you need insurance. But that doesn't mean you need to pay more than you need to. Shopping around for insurance isn't the most fun thing you could have on a Saturday. So maybe do it on a Monday. But do shop around. You can even show a quote to one company and have them match or beat it. Tying in 2 policies together like car and renters insurance can usually get you a deal as well.

The Hack: shop around but don't skimp. Online comparison tools or resources like NerdWallet can help you save and see what you may need vs. what you don't. Driving safely and increasing your deductible on a cheaper-to-insure car is the surest way to save money, of course. But you still don't need to break the bank especially if you find a discount or promotion or even do the math to see that paying by the mile (usage-based insurance) actually is cheaper than paying a flat rate. If you're paying less than $100/month, you're doing better than average.

You know that if someone runs into you, and drives off, you will have to pay your deductible? Not to scare you but this happens all the time. This literally happened to me a couple of months ago. We were enjoying a quiet Sunday morning at home when Crash! Bang! Boom! (or something like that). A delivery truck hit our parked car AND drove off! Without much time to think, I threw on my shoes and yelled out the door, "HEY!!!" That didn't work so I went downstairs to assess the damage. It wasn't too bad, but I knew that I'd have to pay for the damage so what did I do? What any Woke Money Hero would do: I jumped in the car, tracked him down, and confronted him. I don't suggest doing this if the driver seems hostile and I guess looking back I should have called the police. So maybe don't do what I did, but the moral of the story is: I found him, confronted him, and got his information.

When I asked, "Did you hit my car?" He said, "Oh, I thought I hit a rock! I'm sorry!" Hmm...OK. I see it from his perspective: he was likely facing suspension or maybe even termination if he has an accident on his track record. But dude, come on. This is the reason for insurance.

Why this hack hasn't worked for you: are you a careful driver? We all make mistakes and accidents do happen. Please make sure you're properly insured as a driver. Be willing to speak up, shop around, and know the rules when it comes to insurance. You're likely not going to have to use it, but you never know. So it's best to be prepared. But don't pay for something you don't see the value in. Knowing all that you get for your money is key. Do you get discounts on AAA or other roadside assistance? Ask.

PART 5:

Money-Saving Housing Hacks

We've come to the part that is my personal favorite to analyze. I've helped many people understand why saving money and investing in real estate is so lucrative. By renting out property, you're not only paying down the mortgage and getting a write-off on your taxes, but your asset is also appreciating over the years. In addition, if you ever needed a place to live, you've got a built-in insurance policy for housing (and not kicking your tenants out, of course).

CHAPTER 13:

Rent

I'm going to assume that if you're reading a book about saving money that you have not yet realized your dreams of homeownership. This is totally OK. I'm here to help you get on that track if you so wish. The key is to start now. The longer you wait, the more houses tend to cost. So what to do if you're renting and living paycheck to paycheck? Well, if you're living alone, I must kindly ask you to get a roommate. Like now. Actually, like yesterday.

Chances are you already have a roomie. This is good. Unless it's not. Then try getting another roomie or realize that it's only temporary. At this stage in your life, you want to be saving where you can and housing is THE biggest expense you likely have. If you're paying more than 50% of your paycheck to housing, you're screwed. Just kidding. In a larger city, this isn't uncommon. I have 2 guys in my condo right now and for good reason: they wouldn't have been able to afford it on their own.

The Hack: finding a good roomie can sometimes be difficult. But that's not to say that rooming with someone you already know is all rainbows and unicorns. Sometimes small disagreements can escalate quicker with someone you know. What I've found works the best is having things written out in a document you both can reference if questions come up about who's responsible for something or who owes what.

This is similar to what are called bylaws or CC&R's for a condo complex. Since there are multiple people living under one roof, there needs to be a code of conduct so everyone can enjoy their own space. Being clear on bills and when things are due is vital. You don't want to be stuck with a bill and you don't want to inadvertently stick someone with your bill.

Why this hack hasn't worked for you: if you've had a tough roomie situation, you aren't alone. I'm going to have to take a guess that somewhere along the way, you had a miscommunication or a disagreement with how things were supposed to be. If there was a document with the rules laid out, you might have been able to work things out smoother. No guarantees but always worth a shot next time around.

Having a roomie is the surest way to start saving money. Taking it one step further, if you and your landlord are so inclined, you could rent out your apartment on Airbnb when you or your roomie are out of town (with their permission, of course). Your landlord would likely allow it if you give him some of the profit. I personally know people who have been able to do just this. And it's a win-win. But not all landlords are up for it as it increases the traffic of people in and out of the building. It doesn't hurt to ask (unless your landlord is mean then I don't know what to tell you except that sucks and I'm sorry).

CHAPTER 14:

Furniture

What good is an apartment without kickass furniture? Well, you know I'm not about to suggest you go look through the latest issue of the Pottery Barn catalog. But what if you could find Pottery Barn for free?

The Hack: sites like Craigslist or Nextdoor (image above) provide a way for your neighbors (people similar to you, right? You like living in the same place at least) to buy and sell their stuff. The image shows just 4 of the Pottery Barn items currently up on my Nextdoor app. There were plenty more. If you've ever sold something on one of these sites, you know you start high and then always come down in price.

One way to buy for cheap is to first act like you aren't all that interested. Then say something to the effect of "heck, I guess I could go check it out." You're implying that you're doing them a favor. The real trick is to spot a flaw. It could be ever-so-small but you noticed it and you saw other items online that didn't have that flaw. At this point, the seller may get nervous that they won't be able to sell their item for what they wanted and they will be willing to negotiate hard. Just make a mental note that this trick doesn't work ALL the time. One place you really could get a ton of deals is an estate sale.

Estate sales are great ways to find furniture for cheap. The families are likely trying to get rid of a bunch of furniture all at once and may not even be all that savvy on how much everything should cost. This is where making deals happens. The more you throw into the pie of items you're looking to purchase, the more likely the family will want to make you a deal. Put yourself in their shoes. Their main goal is to get rid of stuff.

If you need to buy new furniture, may I suggest a site like Wayfair? This one is great because it has lower-priced items but they're more unique than a big box store like Ikea. Funny story: I was looking for a dining table with my then fiance and we happened upon a warehouse store that boasted the "best prices". Unfortunately for them, quickly researching prices nowadays is all too easy and I quickly found the exact same table for hundreds of dollars less on Wayfair (plus free delivery!). I'm not trying to put retail stores out of business with this suggestion but if it's cheaper online, I simply can't do it.

Why this hack hasn't worked for you: do you like to negotiate or does the idea make you scream? Negotiation is a very handy skill to have especially in the corporate world. You must use it tactfully but if you're able to pull it off, you just got free money. Well, maybe it costs a little blood, sweat, and tears, but you catch my drift.

I remember getting my second real job: a dear friend of mine gave me some tips to negotiate a better offer and looking back, I'm so glad that I did. I had 2 competing job offers but technically you don't need 2 to pull this off. Here's the trick: you say, "I'm surprised that your offer came in ($10K) under my lowest acceptable offer." And then YOU STOP TALKING. This will cause an uncomfortable silence and let me tell ya: it's uncomfortable! I held my breath and didn't say a word and the hiring manager fell all over herself trying to come up with the right response to put my mind at ease. You see, when it comes time to negotiate salary (or anything for that matter), you're in the driver's seat. The company wants something you can provide. You may not be interested if they can't meet your needs.

A word of caution: if I hear of anyone using this tactic and not getting the job, I'd be forever sad. Please use your discretion in what you say and how much you ask for. If you mentioned that your salary requirement was $60K, don't pretend it's $70K (unless of course the requirements for the job change). All I ask is that you practice. It's easy to flub this one but hot damn, did it work well!

CHAPTER 15:

Supplies

This is another one of my favorites simply because, over the years, I've gotten really good at spotting deals and knowing what things should cost. This doesn't have to take a ton of time: before going out shopping, just head on over to a couple sites and compare prices on items that you want to buy. If there's a sale at Home Depot but Lowe's has the item cheaper, you know that you'd probably be wasting your time going to Home Depot. They don't typically negotiate their prices. One exception: you can get amazing deals on open box items. I literally have a rock garden in my side yard that cost all of $5 by using only bags of rocks that had been previously opened. If I had purchased them at the original cost, it would have been closer to $50. Woo hoo.

The Hack: I'm not going to give you a recipe for how to make homemade cleaning supplies (vinegar is like the Woke Money Hero of cleaning btw). There are plenty of sites for that. I will tell you that there are even more "secret" places to buy household items. One such place is the local library. Hear me out: some libraries have tool libraries. I kid you not. They rent out tools and then once they get too many items donated, they sell them. I picked up an electric chainsaw and cut down a tree. Saved $300. Cleaning up was another story. But I'll still consider it a success.

Let's say you're more into the finer things in life besides tools. You want clothes and lots of them. Aside from the usual hack of just shopping at a used clothes store, you might have seen online options popping up. Companies like ThredUP have brought second-hand clothes to a new level while adding the convenience of online shopping. Think about it: instead of going to one store, you're accessing a huge warehouse of second-hand clothes just like you would by shopping online at a regular retail store.

Where you save even more is by buying on sites like Wish which import from China directly. If you weren't aware, thousands of products on Amazon are "dropshipped" from China manufacturing sites like AliExpress and Alibaba. Entrepreneurs use these sites to then mark up the costs and advertise them to consumers on social media and Etsy sites. Why pay for their advertising? Once you know these sites exist, you can do your own shopping. All the latest gadgets are there because it's literally the same site that dropshippers get their supplies from. It's true that sometimes they can get large quantity discounts and you could possibly save money that way if they choose to not include a markup but they will always need to pass on the cost of advertising to you one way or another so make sure to check the shipping cost.

Why this hack hasn't worked for you: if you don't find comparison shopping fun, you may be suffering from analysis paralysis. The stress of finding "the best" deal can be overwhelming. Just look at how popular Black Friday has become: thousands of people braving the cold and waking up in the wee hours of the morning just to find the "best" deals. To help you navigate these deals, there are sites out there that do the comparing for you. Make it easier on yourself. And remember that you're doing more than what most people are when it comes to saving money so give yourself a pat on the back even if you do end up spending a bit more than you thought you should. You'll make up for it in the dozens of other hacks in this book.

Not knowing the sites that will save you money is a dream killer. There's a reason that Alibaba and AliExpress don't have notoriety in the US. These are foreign companies that don't spend money on advertising in the US because they have paying customers (dropshippers) doing that for them. Once you become woke to this fact, you're playing a whole new ballgame than everyone else. You have the inside track and the hacks that will finally help you win the game of saving money.

Speaking of woke, hop on over to www.wokemoneyhero.com/free-resources for a list of recommended companies to save money with.

PART 6:

Money-Saving Entertainment Hacks

Ah, the weekend. Whether you're about to Netflix and chill with your Bae or party it up with your college pals, there are right ways and wrong ways of spending your time when it comes to saving money. If you like blowing large wads of cash in Vegas every weekend, I'm not sure I'm going to be able to help you. If, on the other hand, you're open to a few suggestions, let's begin.

CHAPTER 16:

Subscriptions

Speaking of Netflix and chill, are you paying for a Net-flix account on your own? I'm hoping you already know what I'm going to say. If you can split the bill between you and your roomie or parents even, you're saving a pretty penny over the course of a year. Come to think of it, you can do the same thing for all your subscriptions (if it's allowed, of course). Hulu, cable (if there's an online streaming component), Amazon Prime. It's all the same: they either haven't figured out how to limit usage (they likely have) or they don't want to impose those limits for fear of a backlash.

Either way, right now in history, you can literally save hundreds of dollars a month just by splitting bills. And, of course, you can always splurge every now and again on things like going out to the movies with all the money that you saved. Just skip buying the popcorn and candy there. The way I look at it if I ever get caught bringing my own food into a movie: sometimes I feel hypoglycemic when I don't have sugar (basically I get hangry) so if they ask why I have my own candy, I need it or else I'll faint. No one's ever asked.

The Hack: on things that cost the same regardless of how many people are using them (Amazon Prime is a good example), split the bill!

Why this hack hasn't worked for you: maybe you're already doing this for some subscriptions but not on others. Why? Are you scared to suggest it? Trust me: people aren't thinking about this kind of stuff. But if you suggest it, they'd be all in. That's the kind of responsibility that comes with being a Woke Money Hero, my friend.

CHAPTER 17:

Weekends

Let's say it's a "go big or go home" kind of weekend. How are you going to make your weekend lit without blowing out your wallet? Let's take the example of a birthday weekend. It's your big day and your friends are ready to par-tay. Where do you want to go? What do you want to do? Will it be dinner and tickets to a basketball game? Is that something that you'd want to do for all your friends on their birthday? That can certainly add up.

Adding that up real quick: let's say 10 friends at $100 a ticket (including you). Crap. What about a weekend getaway at an Airbnb for just a couple hundred bucks? Obviously, there can't be a wild party but what if the Airbnb had a projector and you could watch the game on a big screen throwing back a few beers and not worrying about driving anywhere? Order pizza instead of going out to eat. Might sound boring to you now but let me assure you: this sounds like a dream once you have kids. It's the memories that will last a lifetime.

The Hack: if you're spending a bunch of money on an experience that you can have for cheaper, I urge you to at least scale back. Concerts are a great example. I love seeing my favorite bands, groups, and DJ's. But too much of a good thing and the likelihood I just blew $70 on a mediocre performance goes up. Sporting events, same thing. Nothing beats the thrill of being there in person but going too often and it's become an expensive habit.

Why this hack hasn't worked for you: there are experience junkies out there who thrive on doing and experiencing things in the moment. They tend to focus on the here and now which is great. They aren't stuck in the past. They just aren't focused on the future as much. If you blow all your money now, you won't have any for the future. It's a tough lesson to learn. And some just don't want to learn it. But you need to turn your FOMO into JOMO. The joy of missing out will help you save up for those once-in-a-lifetime experiences.

CHAPTER 18:

Holidays

Whether the holidays are a time that you look forward to or a time that you dread, you usually have to come up with a present or 2 (or 12) to give a friend or family member. And it can be tempting to get the most expensive thing you can to prove that you love them but do me a favor and remember the last gift you got: are you using it right now? Every single day? OK, if it was a Kindle or a laptop, you totally schooled me. But I'm guessing for most of you, it wasn't something that you desperately needed. What if people who were trying to figure out what you wanted knew what you wanted and those things were all the things that you needed? Wouldn't that help you to not have to buy as much stuff during the year? Like what if you did need a laptop and you found a refurbished one on Amazon, added it to your wishlist, and casually mentioned it to your Mom. You never know who may be hoping to get you something special unless you put it out there.

And when it comes to buying gifts, who says you have to buy anything? What if you made gifts instead? OK,

I see your point: if you get a laptop and you give a handmade ornament, it's not exactly equitable. Those aren't the best examples. But what if you got a Kindle and you gave a day of chores so your parents could go out for a night on the town and come back to a clean house? The possibilities are endless:

- Bake a couple dozen ultra gooey cookies from an old family recipe for a neighbor
- Make your own gift basket with different types of soaps, lotions, and candles for your Aunt
- Give a coupon for babysitting or pet sitting to a friend
- Offer to assemble or refinish the furniture that you knew another family member just got

The Hack: when you think about why we give presents around the holidays in the first place, it really is to show people that you care. If they're expecting an expensive gift for the simple fact that they want you to spend money on them, that may be a great opportunity to show them that you care even if you aren't spending a ton of money on them. I'd be surprised if someone refused your cookies and demanded a box of Godiva instead.

Why this hack hasn't worked for you: if you're prioritizing things over people, things over saving, you're not likely to want to venture into the realm of giving homemade gifts. But I promise it isn't as scary as you think. It really does show you care. Get creative. You know your peeps better than me. Maybe they're into saving money and they need a copy of this book ;)

All kidding aside, the reason the holidays have turned into a money-making affair is because bottom line: we all want to be happy. And the holidays are supposed to be the "happiest time of the year". Merriment has been exchanged for consumerism. Buying things are supposed to make us happy, right? Wrong. I can tell you from experience: having anything and everything that I could possibly want (my Dad would go to Toys R Us and walk down the aisle at Christmas time throwing things left and right into the cart, coming home with a car full of presents. Santa? No – he told me there was no Santa at age 6. He provided all those presents and wanted me to know the truth) and then having all those things taken away from me, I know that things don't make you happy.

YOU can make yourself happy by focusing on the connections you have in your life and identifying the ways you can give back to those around you. Trust me on this one: you won't remember the things you had or the things you bought, you'll remember how you felt when spending time with loved ones or when you gave a gift to someone who really wanted it or you helped someone who really needed it.

PART 7:

Money-Saving Travel Hacks

Speaking of the holidays, it can actually be a great time to travel. Just make sure the place you're going to isn't underwater because of all the rain or too cold to enjoy outside. I'm guessing this is a favorite category for a lot of you. Without further ado, here you go:

CHAPTER 19:

Points Cards

If you're an avid traveler, you need a points card. Let me rephrase that: it would be smart of you to get one. Why? Because you can literally get where you're already going for free. Not for 20% off or buy one, get one. There are cards out there right now wanting to give you hundreds of thousands of points which equal FREE trips.

The Hack: I've gone around the world on points. Most recently, just to Puerto Vallarta. We stayed at an all-inclusive resort for free for my birthday. It was amazing. And did I mention free? Some cards do have annual fees so if you want to get around that, there are sites that list out all the cards and compare all their features. There are also blackout periods for some cards where you can't book the tickets you may want so be sure to read the fine print before signing up for one of these. If done right though, you are in for a treat.

Why this hack hasn't worked for you: hope you have a credit card. This is the easiest way to build up your credit. Credit is used to qualify for things like car and home loans. So if you have a credit card, there really isn't any harm in having 2. Of course, don't run up a huge bill that you can't pay. You should only be charging things that you know you can pay back. My Mom taught me that lesson when I went off to college. Thanks, Mom.

CHAPTER 20:

Airfare

Aside from a points card, the other way to get cheap airfare is to keep an eye out for deals. Setting up flight alerts lets you tailor the deals that you see and lets you be the first to jump on the opportunity. If you have flexibility in your dates or times, you're in the driver's seat if looking passively online. The boldest thing you can do is take the deal when the airline overbooks your flight and needs to bump someone. That usually includes a voucher for a free flight. Cha-ching.

The Hack: if you know someone who works for an airline, hit them up. They usually have a ton of freebies that they want to give away. I used to fly standby for free in college because my Mom's old roommate from college worked at Southwest. I certainly wasn't too proud to take her up on her offer. The other way to find cheap deals, of course, is an aggregator site like Google Flights. Knowing when to book is key. Tuesdays are typically good. And there is a window of opportunity: it can range from 3 weeks to 3 months in advance for domestic flights.

Why this hack hasn't worked for you: have you ever asked for your seat to be upgraded to business or first class? What's stopping you? I've tried it. They said "No". But at least I tried! I'm going to keep trying until one day they say "Yes!" I know it'll happen. I believe it. If you never ask, you'll never know what could have been.

CHAPTER 21:

Lodging

Travel brings with it surprising memories and often-times surprising bills. Booking a hotel "off the beaten path" can sometimes increase spending by needing to travel to these remote locations. Just something to keep in mind as you start researching places to book your next big trip. Let's look at how to do things the right way.

The Hack: Remember the last amazing trip you took? Maybe it's been a while. What kind of things do you remember the most? Was it the food? Was it the things you did? Or was it the pillow you slept on? Our memories are influenced by our feelings so if we had a great time doing things on a trip, we may not remember the fact that we paid too much for a hotel room or that it rained for 2 days while we were there. If we take that same reasoning, we aren't as likely to remember the bed we slept in (as long as it's comfy enough) and instead focus on having the experiences we want to have.

I've slept in my fair share of hostels through the years,

saving a ton of money. Money that I put towards having kickass experiences, with Instagram pics to prove it. Another hack, if you're up for it, is to sleep on your transportation to another destination. This will allow you to cover more terrain without having to pay for both travel and lodging at the same time. I've made airports, planes, and trains comfortable. A pillow or rolled up sweatshirt goes a long way. Most people don't know, but if there are empty seats on a plane and you ask the flight attendants nicely, you can almost certainly grab the seats and stretch out after takeoff. Don't wish you had asked 4 hours into an 8-hour flight.

Why this hack hasn't worked for you: maybe you're into more accommodating accommodations. That's totally fine. There are plenty of sites that will get you good deals. Just make sure you know what you want. We recently booked a trip to the Maldives and, if you've never been, you'd think that there were only a few options. But let me tell ya: there are hundreds of options to choose from. And thankfully many reviews to read. But if you were to consider every option, you'd quickly become overwhelmed. By using the Search Filter on a site like Booking.com, you can narrow everything down way further by what you really want: things like proximity to city center, all-inclusive, activities, price, beds, and ratings.

Solely relying on what others say just doesn't cut it anymore. Not for a Woke Money Hero like yourself. What others want you may not necessarily want. Being smart about where your money goes is so important. Is it really worth it to get the all-inclusive deal? How much food are you really going to eat on vacation? What if it's super hot outside? We tend not to eat as much. Just look at the pricing and break it down realistically. If there's access to a corner store where you're staying, why not pick up some fruit as breakfast and a snack for later? You may not want an all-you-can-eat buffet every morning. Or worse, you may get it and think you have to eat that much food to feel like you are getting your money's worth. Blah.

Another option that I would be remiss if I didn't mention (and this is certainly not for everyone) is house swaps. You go stay in someone's house while they stay at your house. The coordination can be tough on dates but if you're a little bit flexible, this can literally save you thousands. Or, if you're into pets, there are sites that cater to travelers where you can stay at people's houses for cheap if you take care of their pets while they're away. Why not make your own post to do this on a local forum? Safety is key whenever you're staying in a new environment. That's why sites like this will boast that they run background checks on all their users. But you can never be too sure. Reviews can even be fake so do your due diligence and make sure any red flags are addressed or politely decline the offer.

Last but certainly not least, you could rent out your apartment on Airbnb while you're away. As mentioned, your landlord may not be all for this. You could double check to see if there's a sublease clause. If there is, you may be out of luck, but if your landlord is open to the idea, you could say that there would be a one-time traveler staying in your unit for X number of days only and they will be paying you X amount of money. Landlords always like to know what's going on at a high level, not necessarily all the details (like where the traveler is from, what their name is, etc.). By not boring them with details and being up-front with them, offer to throw in a little extra rent. You may be surprised at how they react. Plus, you're paying for a good portion of your trip. Hopefully, it's a win-win situation. Again, make sure you feel comfortable with who is staying at your place. We've managed an Airbnb for a few years and we always have someone meet the guests. This may not be feasible for you but it sets the tone that we are people who care for our guests and want them to have a great experience. We expect the same in return from our guests.

PART 8:

Budget Hacks

Ah, another one of my favorite topics: budgeting. I know this likely isn't a favorite topic of yours and that's great. Let me do the heavy lifting and you follow along with an open mind. This will be painless.

CHAPTER 22:

Keeping Tabs on Bills & Taxes

Maybe you've tried to keep a budget before and kept it up for a while. That's great. Maybe this is the first time you're tackling the task. If you don't think you need to budget because you don't make much money, this couldn't be further from the case. Likewise, if you're making the big bucks but don't seem to have any left over at the end of the month, budgeting is also for you. The truth is, everyone needs to have some sort of a budget, even the Warrens, Bills, and Marks of the world. Going into debt and not being able to pay it back brings debt collectors, bankruptcy, ruined credit, and wage garnishment. Yikes.

The Hack: If you're old school, I've created a budget worksheet that you can access by signing up on my site: WokeMoneyHero.com. For everyone else, there are free apps that help you budget like Wally and Mint. It doesn't really matter how you do it, just that you do it and fully understand why you have to. That's where I come in.

Think about it: if you could shoot some hoops with an NBA star, would you obsess over what kind of shoes you were wearing? Or what brand of basketball you had? Pretty sure it wouldn't matter to a pro basketball player. Steph Curry is going to steal that ball and make you jump higher than you ever thought you could but he's still going to score on you blindfolded. It's all about what gains you make. However small. If you were playing HORSE with Steph and you beat him without him scoring any points, pretty sure you would make the cover of the NY Times because he likely injured himself or you're DeMarcus Cousins reading my book (if you don't know basketball, these are all pro basketball players). How would you feel if you even scored a point on Curry? Betting you'd at least Tweet about it. And why not? It's a "small" win, but it's a huge win when you realize the stakes!

Most people are happy to dream about what their life would be like if they had a lot of money. But not everyone is willing to do the things necessary to get there. Take the small steps, celebrate those wins. Each move you make toward your goal is closer than you were the day before. It's never too late to start and the sooner you do, the sooner you're able to realize those dreams.

The easiest way I can describe budgeting is that all you're really doing is looking at your life: what you spend money on and what you need to live. That's the easy part. Where things get tricky (and where most people lose track) is when the unexpected pops up. Maybe you forgot about your Aunt's Birthday and to make it up to her, you take her out to a fancy (read: expensive) restaurant. I see 3 things here:

1. By setting up a budget at the beginning of the year and reevaluating it at the start of every month, you're able to better remember and plan for all expenses like Birthdays.

2. Feeling that you have to make things up to people by spending money is simply not necessary. Plus, by being more in control of your expenses, you likely won't have as many unexpected expenses popping up, thus letting you plan ahead for your dollars spent like gifts.

3. Fancy things don't necessarily need to have expensive price tags. Your Aunt would probably still love you the same if you said you were going to cook her a special dinner of her favorite foods. A special touch is worth more than you think.

Why this hack hasn't worked for you: there are an infinite number of reasons to not budget: "it's too hard", "it hasn't worked", "I can't stick to it". But there's one very good reason to budget: you need to be in control of your money in order to save it. Let's examine the complaints above and I will show you why they're BS:

- "Too hard": setting up automatic amounts that you can spend on certain things is actually easy. Have an account at a bank? Did you know that it's likely free to set up another one? By having 2 accounts, you can set up a certain amount to transfer every month from your Savings to your Checking. Need $200 for food every month? By putting in $50 a week, you make it easier on yourself to save in shorter time periods. Putting $200 in all at once and you're more likely to blow it in the first week because your brain thinks that that's all available to you now. Your brain wants to maximize your happiness but remember that saving money is just as fun as spending it once you see this system starting to work.

- "Hasn't worked": getting a low balance fee or a monthly service fee hit is no fun. I've been guilty of one of these at various times in my life and I was probably more hard on myself than I needed to be. But oh did I learn my lesson! Bank fees should be avoided at all costs. Having a reserve account is a must. Most advisors say you should have at least 6 months of living expenses just in case the worst should happen to you. It sucks but it's a reality we're all living with. Monthly service fees can usually be avoided by having qualifying deposits or a certain number of debit card transactions. Make sure you know the rules and the calendar timeline that they use to assess the fees. They have to tell you by law. Super important and trust me, you'll be so far ahead of everyone else when you become conscious of where your money is going. Banks make money off of the interest that they charge on loans and credit cards as well as bank fees. Don't get hit from both sides.

And another thing about budgeting for the big events in your life: most people won't start saving for a house or a wedding until the time comes and they need to move or they find their life partner. But why are they waiting to save? If you know that you will buy a house and will get married, why aren't you saving now? It's not like the expense is going to magically not be there when you want to take the next step. That mentality will keep you stuck right where you are.

I'm going to briefly talk about taxes because my friends and family members have all asked me at one time or another to do their taxes. While I'm not a tax preparer by trade, I've learned a ton of hacks along the way. Paying someone to do your taxes makes sense once you start investing money. But I'm guessing that a lot of you are just starting out and this may not be the case just yet. Totally cool. You have time to learn to do your taxes yourself!

"Um...say what?!" You heard that correctly – you can do your taxes yourself. There is a plethora of online tax software out there that walks you through the process every step of the way. Some are free to prepare your federal taxes and then charge you a nominal fee to file your state taxes. It's ok to pay a little if it saves you hours of work re-inputting numbers on 2 different sites. I remember going into H&R Block after I bought my condo and thinking "I just spent $800 for someone to do my taxes, but I probably could have done them

on my own." That was after a number of years doing my own taxes so I understand if you don't feel comfortable doing them on your own. Just try it. It really isn't as complicated as you think. You can always prepare them and not file if you think you want someone to review them first.

Another hack is writing off your charitable donations. I doubt very much that there is a rich person out there not writing off their charitable donations. You have to pay taxes so why not allocate that money to a charity instead? This is yet another way to take back control of your money. When you start investing, the real write-offs come into play: at the time of this book's publication, you can still write off things like a portion of your mortgage interest and your property taxes. Those things add up over time.

CHAPTER 23:

Staying on Track

You can do it! Promise. That little voice in the back of your head saying it's too hard/hasn't worked is easy to listen to. Staying on track is the hard part once you get going. This whole section is devoted to keeping your eyes on the prize, your heart in the right place, and your goals aligned with your destiny. Cheesy cliches? Sure. Bad ideas? No.

The Hack: the more we save, the more we earn. Ever think about how people start saving money? Were they younger than you? Maybe. Were they doing anything differently than you? Not really. People all have to start somewhere. That first dollar that you consciously tell yourself is not going to be spent because you choose to save it; it will want to be spent for sure. But you won't allow it. You have bigger plans for it even if, like clock-work, you were spending those bucks before.

Remember me asking you what YOU really want? This is the time to get really clear about what that is. Is it saving enough for a down payment on a house? Buying a new car? (That was a trick question). Staying in the most expensive over-priced hotels? (Another trick question). I don't mean to make light of your dream whatever IT is that your heart desires – I want you to have it. I want you to picture yourself with it every day. What will the future look like once you get it? How will you feel?

Why this hack hasn't worked for you: sticking to something isn't easy. Especially when we've been pro-grammed our whole lives to spend money to be happy. Making things easier on yourself with automatic de-posits, having a reserve amount, and with your big goal in mind, you'll be able to take back control of your money.

Think of saving money like losing weight: you need to decrease the input more than the output. We may know this objectively but we still continue to pack on the pounds or we keep spending money. What's one proven way to lose weight? Besides getting gas-tric bypass surgery, have you ever had an important event that you needed to look good for? A wedding or a reunion? Well, with saving money, you also have im-portant events to look forward to: owning a house, for example. We'll need to shed a few pounds (expenses) in order to reach our goal faster. It's making sure that goal is crystal clear in our minds as something we want to attain for it to work.

That being said, at the end of the book, there's a free gift for you to help you out with staying on track. Be sure to check it out! (after you read the rest of the book, of course).

CHAPTER 24:

Investing

Once you've started actually saving money, what are you going to do with that money? Well, you could let it sit there and get it out once you need it to buy whatever goal you have in mind. Or, you could put that money to work for you. We come to the chapter that teaches you to make your money work for you instead of you working for your money. This is the point where you really start to understand how the rich operate.

If you told most people that you are starting to invest your money, what do you think they'd say? I think it would be something along the lines of, "What stocks are you buying?? I want in too!" I'm not a stock broker so I'm not going to give you ANY stock help. Rather, there is another investment that I think is really worth your time. It only has 3 letters: **_YOU_**. That's right: the best investment you can make is yourself. You know yourself better than anyone else so you know what you like, what you don't like, and what your strengths are. Don't let someone else tell you what you should like or be into. That's a personal choice. I'm simply saying that investing in learning more about what you like can make you money.

Take me for example. From an early age, I was into real estate. Why? Because my Dad was into it and I wanted to be like him. I didn't question it at the time. I just knew that I liked it. So then I got good at it: observing what my parents did to operate hundreds of apartment units and a couple office parks. It was a TON of work. And I didn't see my Dad for a lot of the time. So my experience formed my opinion: real estate can make you a lot of money but if you don't make it easy enough to operate, you won't be able to spend time with your family. And look at what happened: my Dad made a few bad investments that caused him to lose it all. My life has revolved around how to keep money close. I'm completely aware and in control of it. My past experience has caused me to have a skewed view of needing to keep it close. But that fact is actually helping me teach you about and help you to understand your own attachment to money which is likely nowhere near as OCD as mine. That's great. We're both learning more about how money affects us, both good and bad.

Once you see what you're passionate about, pursue it. Learn everything you can about it and then teach others. The more value you give to others, the more you'll be rewarded. I am just now learning this lesson after years of thinking that a 9-5 job was going to somehow, someday provide that for me. After getting laid off not once. Not twice. But 3 times (!) I know that each time was a lesson in disguise. The first one hurt like crazy. The second was welcomed. And by the third one, I had one foot already out the door.

I knew my "calling" was to invest in real estate and then show others how I did it by saving money. If you're getting a lot of your friends asking you how to do something that comes totally naturally to you, this could be a clue that you're standing on a goldmine. It's hard to see that others may not get what you can see so clearly. It could be mountain biking. You could set up a review site for mountain bike shoes. It could be dogs. You could set up a site for your own dog walking services and market them when you're out walking your own dog. The trick is to invest in yourself. You no longer need someone to tell you what can bring you happiness. You hold the key to unlock that right now.

The Hack: I firmly believe we're at a turning point when it comes to education. The fact that a textbook can be outdated within a matter of months due to technological advances means that online education will only be getting not just more popular but more essential. Having a degree and work experience only goes so far. That's why learning new skills online is key these days. And one of those keys is how to make money online as a side hustle or full-time gig. Trust me, the days of "working for someone else" in a traditional sense will get less and less popular and be less and less necessary.

There are so many "gurus" out there that you could take

online courses with who will teach you how to make money online with things like dropshipping and Amazon FBA. I actually watched 30 free webinars on "how to make money online" during the course of figuring out my plan to write this book and 2 of them provided value. I guess if I combined all 28 others, there was some value there too. What's interesting is that someone else watching all 30 of those webinars probably would have gotten something entirely different out of the experience. That's because everyone's different. We all have different strengths and different interests.

Here's probably the most valuable hack I can impart upon you when it comes to making money online: there's no right way to do it, but there is a smart way to do it. The "gurus" who run Facebook ads (you've probably seen them in your Facebook news feed) charge upwards of $2000 per course. I understand why they do it. They're trying to make a living. And I get it. But I don't advise spending all this money. Would it be more valuable than a college education? I'm sorry to say that the answer is maybe. But the fact remains that you have likely already spent a lot on education (that's why I haven't touched on it much until now). But there are ways to get this "making money online" education cheaper than what most people are paying. Oh, boy! Here we go:

- The free webinar that "gurus" provide after you sign up for their list can actually be pretty fun. You can get exposed to dropshipping, Amazon FBA, Shopify. You can see which one you naturally gravitate towards and learn more about the topic on free YouTube educational videos.

- I think I mentioned that I got a course for free. I basically reached out and said that I could introduce the guru to some of the people I used to work with in the same industry. He was so thankful after the call that he asked if I wanted access to the course. He was happy to do it to "repay" me. I didn't even have to ask for it.

- This one's a little trickier but you could offer a review video of the product in exchange for access to the course. When I tried this one, I got a significant savings of $300, but I didn't pursue it. He was basically telling me he valued my service at $300 which I didn't want to give him the satisfaction of getting. I could have taken it one step further and asked if he would let me be an affiliate of his products but more on that in the next chapter.

Why this hack hasn't worked for you: turning your money from something that you work for into something that works for you is HUGE. It's life-changing. It's the best thing since sliced bread. It's the point at which the scales tip in your favor, allowing you to get out of the rat race. I could go on and on so I'm going to in the next chapter.

And don't forget there are a lot of other online education sites you can get for free – Udemy has free courses on IT and technology, Codeacademy has free coding classes, and Morningstar and Vanguard have free resources on how to invest in stocks.

PART 9:

Making Money Hacks

It's one thing to invest your money. And it's another thing to actually make money. The problem with "guru" courses is that after you spend all that money, you may have learned a thing or two but making more money than what the course cost is tricky. You feel like you spent all this money so you should have learned everything there is to learn. But sorry, no. If you don't adapt and continue to learn new skills as you go, you're going to fail.

CHAPTER 25:

Online Courses

Do not worry, my friend. I saved the best hack for this section. Which is simply that there are sites out there that have realized there is a huge demand for these courses but not everyone has $2000 lying around. What they've geniusly (is that a word? It should be!) done is crowdsourced the info and made it available for a monthly fee. You can also purchase access to individual courses. I think it's genius. Some of you may be thinking: "Won't the owners of these courses be pissed that people can get access to their courses so cheap?" I asked my friend who has a course and he said that he expects people to find his courses for cheap. What he's really selling is access to him and his knowledge. Most gurus worth their salt will answer questions if you email them.

Well, let's see: I just told you that the information can be found for free (don't steal it) or cheaper than what others are spending. And I told you literally everything I know about how to save money and invest it. You're so many light years ahead of others that my head is exploding. You literally know more than every one of your friends at this point. Legit Woke Money Hero territory here.

The Hack: Google "free online marketing courses." These won't be from the flashy gurus you see online but that's OK. The gurus are trying to sell you on the dream of becoming rich and famous. I can assure you it's part of the image they want to project. Even a lot of celebrities are trying to sell you on the dream. They only promote what they think you will consume. Think about it: would you rather learn from someone who's trying to sell you on what they think you want to hear or someone who genuinely wants to help you? Don't get tricked into thinking that you need to learn tactics from people who spend huge amounts of money on advertising and show you their expensive cars and houses. There's a reason they do that and it's not to "help people". They make their money off of selling courses on how to make money.

Speaking of courses created to actually help people, I created a course if you're interested. It takes the concepts of what I'm teaching here and provides visual elements to drive the points home. Think of it as your secret savings weapon. Of course, it's extremely affordable. You can find it on my site www.wokemoneyhero.com.

Why this hack hasn't worked for you: you haven't looked for other ways to get those high priced courses before. It is possible to get the information that you need cheaper and literally change your life over the course of a few weeks. I can't tell you how invaluable this one little hack is. Please don't pass this opportunity up. If I've provided value to you with all the hacks in this book, please know that this hack is the biggest.

And maybe you haven't even heard of any of these online "gurus" yet. Just know that there are many, many people out there right now who have caught on to the fact that they can charge people to teach them how to make money online. Some of these teachers know what they're doing and can provide value to you. But there are so many people out there who are out to make a quick dollar and not really provide any long-term value.

It saddens me to think that there are people struggling to make rent and think that spending (or charging) $1,000 on a Making Money Online course will solve all their problems. Worse yet are the people who prey on these people.

CHAPTER 26:

Websites

So you've saved some money and started investing in yourself by learning a valuable skill. You've learned that you want to start an online business with passive income. That's great. You can put in some work at the beginning and watch the dollars roll in. There are a number of ways to do this but I've found (you guessed it) the cheaper way to do it. I take you through the process in my entirely free course by signing up for my newsletter at WokeMoneyHero.com. That being said, since you've already learned so much, I'm going to share some hacks now that I've piqued your interest.

The Hack: in order to get your online business humming, you're going to need a website. And maybe not just one website but several. Buying domain names is super easy and cheap. Sites like HostGator and Namecheap or GoDaddy all do the same thing: they allow you to register a domain. But then you'll need to host it. You'll accomplish a number of things by hosting several domains with the same company: ease of monitoring and lower cost with the ability to "add on" domains.

An "add on" domain literally means: add a domain for free. This is huge and isn't a well-known concept. What I'm telling you is that you can have 20 domains and host them all under 1 hosting plan. Do you see the possibilities here? Do you see where I'm going? The more sites you have, the greater the likelihood that you'll succeed. This is where 99% of people fail. They think that they'll make money online with a site and if that site doesn't work, they give up. They were so close! They could have applied what they learned to help them grow their online business in whatever form that eventually takes on, but they stopped dead in their tracks not realizing the goal was within their reach if they had only reached a little. Bit. Further.

Why this hack hasn't worked for you: if you've heard all the "gurus" say how easy it is to make money online, or maybe they were real with you and told you it takes time and effort, and you tried to do it yourself and saw that it's hard and gave up, it's time to try with all the skills you've learned in this book. Think about the person you were before you started reading and the person you are now. You've come far, believe me. Much farther than others who are clueless to this stuff. Having the mindset to now take on money and show it who's boss.

CHAPTER 27:

Affiliate Marketing

Remember the 30 webinars that I watched? Well, I learned that Affiliate Marketing was where it's at. From my experience, it's the easiest, least expensive way to make money online. And there are a ton of free courses and ways to get at the real gurus (like I mentioned above).

I do have to make the disclaimer: there are different ways to make money online and some are going to appeal more to others. I'm an introvert so didn't want something that required me to go out and sell. If that's you, more power to you. You have to do you. You see, at one of my last 9-5 jobs, I was doing email marketing so the natural next step in my entrepreneurial journey was to have an email list where I could create value for my readers. I sincerely hope that I've done that for you, emails or not.

The Hack: the trick to affiliate marketing is that you're the relationship manager between a company's product and its potential customers. An Affiliate Marketer is a bridge between the two. They're really good at showing why a product is a good bet and how it can solve a problem for the consumer. I get to do this all day, every day. Regardless of whether or not I'm actually "working". This is the power of passive income. While all your friends are working for a living, you're living to work because you love it so much. It's a crazy concept and one you won't fully grasp until it happens to you. But you'll definitely know when it does.

Why this hack hasn't worked for you: I think the misconception of Affiliate Marketing or Marketing, in general, is that people use shady tactics in order to promote products or make a sale. While that may be true for some, it's the exception rather than the rule.

When you think about it, everything is Marketing. Need a date? You better present yourself right or that's not going to happen much. Want a better job? Of course you need to have the skills but someone who markets themselves better will surely get it over the person who "wishes" it would happen. Marketing is just a bridge to getting what you want in a more efficient way. Have a great product but no one buying? Your marketing's off. Wrote a great book that no one's reading? You didn't promote it correctly. Knowing the right hacks makes all the difference.

With the hacks that I've presented to you and why they may not have worked for you before, I hope that I've provided every cent of value to you. If you're interested in making money online, I have a free training on my website called "Become an Affilaite". Here's the link:

http://www.wokemoneyhero.com/becomeanaffiliate

As an added bonus, I wrote 3 more chapters to help you save when it comes to major life events: throwing a wedding (or major party), getting a dog (or cat), and having a baby (or two). And remember, signing up for my email newsletter gets you the free course on how to make money online the easiest (and cheapest) way possible.

PART 10:

Bonuses

BONUS 1:

"Throwing" a Wedding on the Cheap

So you've met the love of your life. Congrats! I'd like to take this opportunity to thank you for entrusting me with the unbelievably big responsibility of helping you plan this wedding. Big breath. It's going to be awesome. First things first. Let's set a budget. I'm the first to tell you that you can have an amazing wedding for $20K in an expensive city. I know because I did. But if you have help from your parents, and the budget can be moved upwards, by all means, go for it.

The Hack: much like the travel hacks I mentioned in a previous chapter, you can focus more on the experience than the color of the napkins for example. No one's going to remember your "theme" and most pictures are going to be of you both at the altar (or wherever you say your vows) or tearing it up on the dancefloor. So what's included in this amazing experience? Well, the venue itself, of course.

How do you get a reasonably priced venue you ask?

Have you been to a wedding that you thought, "They must have spent a fortune!" Have you looked up how much it actually cost online? Venues will be more than willing to divulge this information because they don't make money if people aren't booking the venue. My hack involved a venue in a city just outside the major city and in a gorgeous gated park within the city limits that was maybe 10 times cheaper than other high-end venues. Given the location and price, it was known to fill up quickly so I can't stress this enough: book early! Aside from getting the date you want, there could quite possibly be an early-bird special. Doesn't hurt to ask or even say that you were referred by your friend who attended a wedding there last year. Anything to get them thinking that you wouldn't be booking unless there was some prior knowledge of the venue. (Remember, everything is Marketing).

Next up: food. This one is very personal. But there are still ways to get a good pricing option. With this one, you need to shop around. $100 a plate isn't crazy in a large metro area when you think about service and cleanup. We went to 4 tastings and finally decided on a lady who had been doing this for maybe 40 years. Experience matters here. These caterers will know what menu items work and which ones are hardest to provide.

Once you have the venue and the food, the rest is easy peasy. Things like seating, tableware, lights, dance floor, and the sound system can typically be arranged through the venue itself. In terms of flowers, photography, and music, these can all be DIY if you want. You may have a sister or brother-in-law who loves arranging flowers, an Aunt who loves music, or a brother who is a photojournalist. I've found that people are willing and able to help you make your big day extra special and may even be honored that you asked. We went the professional photographer route but chose one who was just starting out so her rates were much cheaper than others but her quality was on-point. We also chose to do online invitations. When was the last time you kept an invitation? Ok, the ladies might but fellas don't usually.

To make the day extra special, I suggest focusing on 3 things: the vows, the MC, and the first dance. These are the things that you'll remember and when you choose to focus on them, you're telling your audience (your family and friends) that you value them and in a weird way that you're making the "show" entertaining. I know thinking about your wedding like a show is a little weird but hear me out. Have you ever been to a boring wedding? Exactly. You know why it was boring? The couple getting married may love each other with all their heart, but if that doesn't come through in the "show", people will remember that feeling. So, take some extra time to make your vows funny/loving/memorable, ask your MC (this can be your BFF or someone you trust) to throw in some jokes or stories about the two of you, and remember to practice the first dance to make it the reason people get on the dance floor to shake their booty.

As an added bonus, you can give party favors to guests as they either arrive or leave the party. I mean wedding :) Some inexpensive options: a poem in a small picture frame, cork stoppers with your initials, M&M's in jars with your faces printed on them (they do this!). You can get super creative here and for a few extra hundred dollars, guests can take home a present with the memories. Don't forget to set up a #hashtag to capture photos for free of your big day. I didn't hit on wardrobe because of how personal a decision it is. Just remember: if it's something that you'll only wear for a day, does it really make sense to drop a $K?

Why this hack hasn't worked for you: most people think that weddings cost a fortune, there aren't any cheaper options for venues, and if you aren't spending enough, your wedding will suck. That thinking is what keeps people poor. I'm living proof that an amazing wedding can happen for less than $20K. And that included part of the rehearsal dinner (thanks to my mother-in-law who picked up most of the tab). This didn't include all the money we got as gifts and used towards our honeymoon. Sites like Zola let you ask for honeymoon funds in lieu of a physical present. Even allowing you to make up things like "dance lessons for my bae" or "romantic dinner at our hotel". The possibilities are endless. Best day ever. Done.

BONUS 2:

Having a Dog on the Cheap

AH, dogs. They're like the little training wheels on your bike ride to having a baby. Get this right in your internship period and the real job of having a job, I mean baby, will be so much easier.

The Hack: "dogs are so expensive". Well, Woke Money Hero, you already know that there are a ton of preconceived notions about this one. Not only is having a dog not expensive, having a dog is the coolest thing you could ever possibly do. I may sound like I'm exaggerating. But you haven't met my dog :)

Where most people think a dog costs a lot of money is the vet. And I've heard that pet insurance can work in your favor. But if you have a relatively young, healthy dog, you likely don't need insurance yet. As long as you're feeding them healthy food and giving them enough exercise and sleep, they shouldn't even need to go to the vet aside from checkups and vaccines. (I'm not a vet and don't claim to be. If your dog has medical issues, insurance may very well be the way to go.)

Speaking of food, we have a little guy, so he obviously eats very little compared to a bigger dog but the same thinking applies: buying in bulk works the same way as it does for human food. The biggest difference (besides the ingredients) is the fact that dry dog food lasts longer for the most part. Am I saying that you need to budget your dog's food? Kind of. You'll know when it's time to get more food. Try making it as predictable as possible: they're likely eating the same amount at each meal and getting fed each day so it stands to reason that they would need new food from the store the same number of days apart each week or month.

Ever notice how when you buy your pup a new toy he plays with it for a while and then either gets bored with it or legit eats it? That's because they're like kids: sometimes simpler is better. They may just want 1 or 2 favorite toys. So no need to go overboard with the spoiling them. You can do that with cuddles. And dollar stores are great for dog toys – no worries when they destroy it. And you can always have extra on hand at those prices.

Have a company with a dog policy? That's awesome. Not only are you able to save on daycare, you get to spend extra time with them. If you can't bring them with you and need to be away for longer than 4 or 5 hours, best to get either a dog door or a dog walker. Post on Nextdoor that you're looking for a reasonably priced walker or scour Rover. One cool way to save is to exchange time with a neighbor. Maybe you work from home on Fridays but need to be in the office on Mondays and your neighbor has the exact opposite schedule. No worries – just watch their dog on Fridays and have them watch yours on Mondays. That way you're using time instead of money. One last hack is getting a remotely operated snack dispenser. These go the extra mile when you can't be home and let you control a snack dispenser from an app in your phone. They also let you check in on your furry friend with a built-in camera.

Why this hack hasn't worked for you: listening to everyone say how expensive a dog is isn't helping you get a dog. They are a lot of work, trust me. But totally worth it!

BONUS 3:

Having a Baby on the Cheap

The biggest life changer is on its way: your new baby. Congrats! It's a very exciting/scary/hopeful/surprising/exhilarating time. Preparation is extra important with this one so make sure you plan ahead for things like child care, furniture assembly, and sleep.

The Hack: I'm not going to give a ton of hacks on caring for a baby because every parent and couple (and in-law) has their own thoughts on what they think is best for the child. I will, however, give you the hacks to save money on caring for a baby. The same theme applies to having children as it does for any major life event: most people will say that "it's so expensive!" And I totally get that 100%. But is there a possibility that there's a cheaper way to do things? I've certainly been there, done that and I didn't spend a fortune.

Let's look at 2 things: the baby's room and childcare. Remember how I said you can get cheaper or even free furniture for your apartment on Nextdoor? Try Craigslist and Facebook Marketplace too. There are many people having babies who spent an exorbitant amount on toys and furniture that the baby grows out of and/or will never use again. They ain't Woke Money Heroes. And these items are in near perfect condition. I'm not saying go out and grab a crib that's falling apart. Nothing could be further from the truth. But what you could do is post that you're looking for specific items like baby clothes and someone may have forgotten that they have a bunch but are willing to part ways with them if they'd be going to a good home.

Child care is one of those things that again is very tied to personal values and opinions. But there are ways to find cheaper alternatives. I personally know a woman who runs a daycare out of her home. She's able to charge less than a daycare that has a large enrollment because she doesn't have a large group of kids. Your little one gets personal attention but you aren't paying for a nanny. There's always the nanny share idea if you're into having a friend's child be included under your nanny's care. If you're so lucky, and your parents live nearby, this could be a temporary solution to having a full-time sitter. Of course, if you work from home, you could always let your friends know that they could leave their kids with you for a few hours for a small fee just to cover food or transportation. Get creative.

Why this hack hasn't worked for you: if you think that your child deserves the best, I agree. Does that necessarily need to cost thousands and thousands of dollars? I don't think so. Especially when they're happier with a tin can over the latest doohickey from the toy store :)

Companies have started catching on that people aren't wanting to spend thousands of dollars on baby supplies. Take, for example, the Shoo Bassinet. These are top-of-the-line and mimic the inside of a womb (or something like that) but within a few weeks or months, parents stop having a use for them. You will find them on Nextdoor for maybe $1000 used. That's because people want to get part of their investment back, of course. So what has the company done? It's started a rental program. This way, they're able to get more profit off of one bassinet. The LTV (long-term value) of each automatically increases. You would simply be adapting this model to fit your needs: finding other items for less or free on Nextdoor with the expectation of recouping your investment at a later date or giving back to the community which supported you in the first place. Either way, you're saving a ton.

CONCLUSION

There you have it, "27+ Hacks to Your Financial Freedom." I told my publisher, "Now the next time someone tells me that I wrote the book on saving money, I can say 'Oh, yeah. I did do that!'" You can also brag to your friends (or parents) that you read a book on saving money and have a plan in place to save up and reach your goal.

We've covered a lot and I want to congratulate for getting through it. And if anyone asks, you can say that you're a Woke Money Hero. Woke Money Hero himself told you.

The 3 biggest takeaways that I have for you as you continue your journey of saving (and making) money:
• Do what others are too scared to do: if the general consensus is that it's "too expensive" to do something, prove them wrong. With all the hacks I've given you, there's a strong possibility that nothing is too expensive. Thinking creatively and having the guts to step just beyond your comfort

zone are 2 ways to tackle this one.

- Saving money is easy: once you set things up to automatically save, you're in control of your money. Anyone can do this, but only a handful actual master it. Once you're saving money, you're able to re-invest in yourself and eventually have your money work for you.
- The cliche of finding what you're good at and what problem the world needs to be solved is true: being a problem solver will bring with it money beyond your wildest dreams if you allow it and never stop learning how to give your gifts to help the world. We need you.

The choice is yours: do you stay stuck in the endless cycle of spending money, making others rich, or do you finally listen to what YOU want and crank your dreams from fuzzy to flossy?

"I see the future when I wake up and it's brighter." -Tep No

WANT MORE?

wokemoneyhero.com

Whoa! It's official – you finished and are 27+ hacks closer to financial freedom. Congrats.

I'm truly grateful that you came on this journey with me so I wanted to hook you up with a special offer!

People come to me all time asking for individual help with their particular money situation but given that I no longer charge for my time, I put together a free e-course for you.

Think of it as having your own personal Money Coach in your back pocket guiding you every step of the way :)

If you want free access to the course I created on the exact steps to turn your newly saved money into passive income, make sure to sign up for my email list. Here's the link to sign up to start making your money work for you:

http://www.wokemoneyhero.com/free-guide/

Here's to more of whatever it is your heart desires!

Cheers,
-Woke Money
Founder of WokeMoneyHero.com

FOOTNOTES

Avatar "Designed by macrovector / Freepik"

IMPORTANT: Earnings and Legal Disclaimers

Earnings and income representations made by Woke Money Hero, wokemoneyhero.com and its advertisers/ sponsors are aspirational statements only of your earnings potential. The success of individuals, testimonials and other examples used are exceptional, nontypical results and are not intended to be and are not a guarantee that you or others will achieve the same results. Individual results will always vary and yours will depend entirely on your individual capacity, work ethic, business skills and experience, level of motivation, diligence in applying the principles set forth on wokemoneyhero.com, the economy, the normal and unforeseen risks of doing business, and other factors.

Wokemoneyhero.com, and Woke Money Hero individually, are not responsible for your actions. You are solely responsible for your own moves and decisions and the evaluation and use of our products and services should be based on your own due diligence. You agree that Wokemoneyhero.com is not liable to you in any way for your results in using our products and services. See our Privacy Policy for our full disclaimer of liability and other restrictions.

Wokemoneyhero.com, including Woke Money Hero personally, may receive compensation for products and services they recommend to you. Woke Money Hero personally uses a recommended resource unless it states otherwise. If you do not want Wokemoney-hero.com and Woke Money Hero to be compensated for a recommendation, then we advise that you search online for the item through a non-affiliate link.

---

[1]   https://www.thebalance.com/components-of-gdp-explanation-formula-and-chart-3306015

[2] Kiyosaki, Robert T., and Sharon L. Lechter. 1998. *Rich dad, poor dad: what the rich teach their kids about money that the poor and middle class do not!* Paradise Valley, Ariz: TechPress.

[3] https://www.cnbc.com/2018/08/28/how-much-money-americans-have-saved-at-every-age.html

[4] https://www.theguardian.com/lifeandstyle/2003/oct/28/healthandwellbeing.health3

www.ingramcontent.com/pod-product-compliance
Lightning Source LLC
Chambersburg PA
CBHW071317220526
45468CB00001B/405